AN
ANNIVERSARY
BLESSING

inscription

AN
Anniversary
BLESSING

MCMXCIX

LAUGHING ELEPHANT

LAUGHING ELEPHANT

POST OFFICE BOX 4399
SEATTLE
WASHINGTON 98104

I ask a Blessing

on the Anniversary

of our Marriage,

and here express

my wishes for its

joyful continuation.

MAY OUR HOME BE A PLACE
WHERE WE ARE
PROTECTED AND NOURISHED.

LET THE SMALL ACTIVITIES
OF OUR DAILY LIVES CONTINUE
AS PLEASING RITUALS,

OFFERING THE SATISFACTION
OF MEANINGFUL REPETITION.

I HOPE THAT THE PLANNING
OF ADVENTURES CONTINUES AS
A REGULAR PART OF OUR LIVES,
AND WHEN THEY OCCUR
LET THEM BE EVEN BETTER
THAN THE ANTICIPATION.

MAY THERE BE FOR US
MANY RICH DAYS TO SAVOR
FROM ROSY SUNRISE
TO GLORIOUS SUNSET,

AND MANY MORE YEARS
TO ENJOY, FROM
DEEPEST WINTER TO FRESH
AND BUDDING SPRING.

LET THERE BE MUCH GOOD
CONVERSATION—

THE JOY OF TALKING DEEP INTO
THE NIGHT, THE EXCITEMENT
OF DIFFERING AND THE
SATISFACTION OF RESOLUTION.

MAY THERE CONTINUE TO BE
AMPLE OPPORTUNITIES
FOR ENRICHING SOLITUDE.

I WISH FOR US
FREQUENT OPPORTUNITIES
TO USE OUR GIFTS
TO CREATE A SHARED BEAUTY,

AND MAY THIS SHARING MAKE
EACH OF US CONTENT
WITH QUIET EVENINGS
AND SIMPLE DAYS.

MAY WE ALWAYS BE AWARE OF
THE EVER-PRESENT WONDERS
OF NATURE, AND TURN
TOGETHER TOWARD THEM.

21

LET US NOT FORGET
THE PROFOUND USEFULNESS OF
PLAY AND NONSENSE.

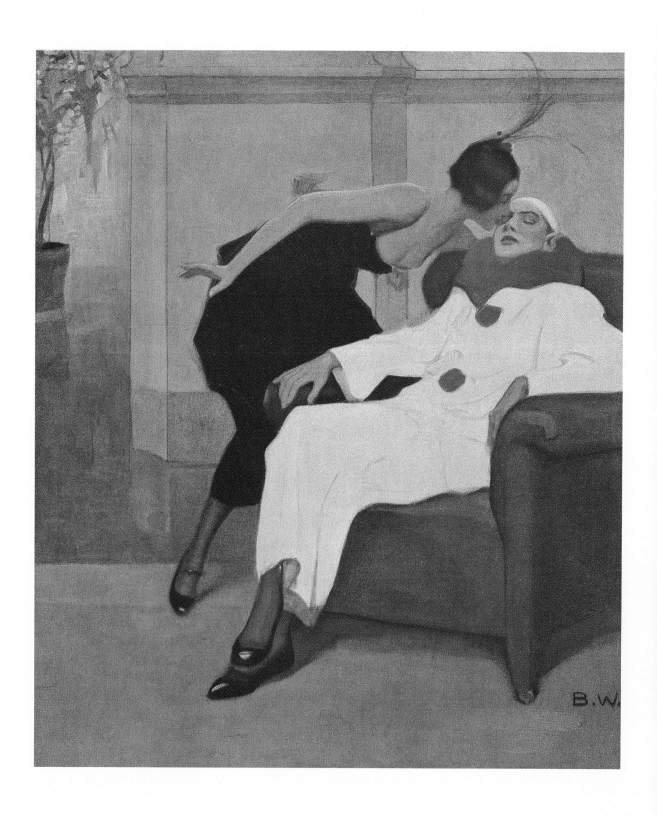

MAY THERE BE MANY MOMENTS
IN WHICH OUR UNITY
CAN BE SILENTLY AFFIRMED.

I WISH FOR US UNCOUNTED
MOONLIT EVENINGS

AND AS MANY
SUN-FILLED MORNINGS.

MAY WE LIVE OUR
LIVES IN ROOMS THAT
REFLECT OUR NATURES
AND OUR ASPIRATIONS.

LET US BE LIKE TREES
STANDING TOGETHER
AGAINST ALL WEATHERS,

GROWING SEPARATELY
BUT NEXT TO ONE ANOTHER.

MAY WE LONG GO ON—

SLEEPING, WAKING, LAUGHING,
PLANNING, REJOICING, WORKING,
RESTING, GETTING, GIVING—
ALWAYS TOGETHER.

P I C T U R E C R E D I T S

PICTURE CREDITS